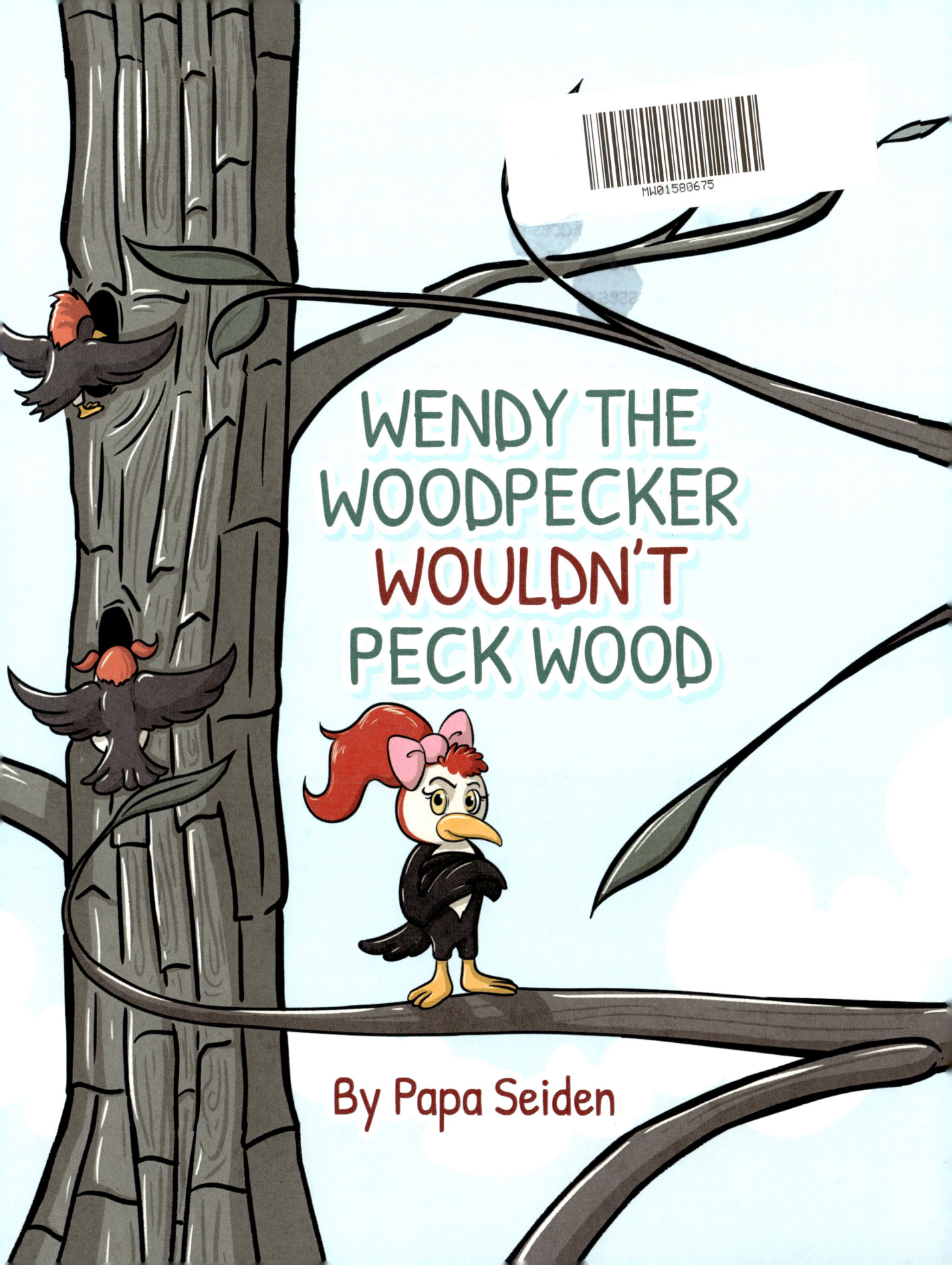

Copyright 2021 Michael T. Seiden

*Wendy the Woodpecker Wouldn't Peck Wood*, is a work of fiction. Names, characters, places and incidents are products of the author's imagination or are used fictitiously. Any resemblance to actual events, locales, businesses or persons, living or dead, is entirely coincidental or used for fictitious purposes only.

All rights reserved.

No part of this publication may be reproduced, distributed or transmitted in any form or by any means, electronic or mechanical methods, including photocopying, recording, or by any information or retrieval systems, without the prior written permission of the author, except in the case of brief quotations embodied in reviews and certain other non-commercial uses permitted by law. The moral right of the author and illustrator has been asserted.

For orders please visit: www.papaseidenstoriesllc.com or Amazon.com

ISBN: 978-1-7368243-0-6 (paperback)
ISBN: 978-1-7368243-1-3 (e-book)
ISBN: 978-1-7368243-2-0 (hardcover)

Cover and book design by: Kezia at GetYourBookIllustrations.
Illustrations by: Marlon at GetYourBookIllustrations.
Project Management by: Nikita Lopes at GetYourBookIllustrations.

First print 2021

Papaseidenstoriesllc.com

# Dedication

This book is dedicated to three women in my life.

First, my mother, who took the eggs I wouldn't eat as a kid, and transformed them into a mish-mosh I loved, and thus was the inspiration for this story.

Second, Regina Barnes, my ninth-grade English teacher who recognized and encouraged the creative imagery in my mind.

And third, my wonderful wife Kathleen, who provided me with love, encouragement and incredible support, all of which helped make this project possible.

Wendy the woodpecker wouldn't peck wood,
Even though she knew she should.

Her mom and dad said, "It tastes good!"
But Wendy had no taste for wood.

Instead of wood she'd often choose
Food from peoples' barbecues.

While others pecked at oak and pine,
Wendy liked your food and mine.

Then she started gaining weight,
Stuffed with all the food she ate.

She couldn't fly from tree to tree,
For Wendy had no energy.

Her mom took her to Doctor Peck,
Who knew exactly what to check.

The doctor said, "Her beak is prickly!
People food has made her sickly."

"She needs wood and little worms,
To keep away the people germs."

"Feed her wood and heed my warning,
She needs sawdust every morning."

"And each evening after dark,
Feed her bugs in cedar bark."

"Doc," her mom said, "I can't feed her Sawdust and those bugs in cedar."

"I can't feed her bugs in wood! She won't eat it, though she should."

So her mother diced and mashed,
Stirring up some wood chip hash.

Mixing sawdust in with water,
Making mush that looked good, sorta.

Then she added whole wheat germ,
Pinch of bug and half a worm.

"Well my dear," was mom's reply,
"Here's a treat you oughta try."

"It's made special, don't ask why,
Warm and mushy, mish-mosh pie!"

Wendy took a little bite,
"Know what mom? I think you're right."

Wendy chewed, "It's kinda sweet,
Tastes like pudding, good to eat!"

Wendy ate, and time passed by,
How she thrived on mish-mosh pie!

Fever gone, her brain alert,
Wendy craved this new dessert.

For her breakfast and for lunch,
Mish-mosh pie is what she'd munch.

Years went by and she grew up,
Slurping mish-mosh from a cup.

Eating mish-mosh was the rule,
While attending birding school.

Other school birds loved it too!
'Specially the mish-mosh stew.

Wendy had a great suggestion,
To her mom she posed this question:

"Could we open fast food diners?-

"Cardinals flying to St. Louie,
Will just love our mish-mosh, gooey."

"As for eagles up from Philly,
We'll prepare some mish-mosh chili."

"As for fly-bys who don't savor
Mish-mosh and its woody flavor-"

"-We'll prepare more varied lunches,
Earthy worms in buns or bunches!"

# About the Author

Michael Seiden grew up in the Bronx, and attended the High School of Music and Art in New York City. He spent many years as a band director, teacher and professional trombonist.

His passion is, and always has been writing, and writing in rhyme. He credits his ninth grade English teacher, Regina Barnes for her encouragement and support, for helping transform him "from a gangly, insecure adolescent, to a gangly, more secure young adult."

He recalls studying Greek Mythology in her English class. The homework assignment was to list and write a few words about each of the Greek Gods. He rhymed them all, but remembers Poseidon:

*The Greecian Poseiden swims better than me,
I'm a mere Seiden, He's God of the Sea!*

All of Papa Seiden's children's books are told in a witty, thoughtful melodic rhyme, including this magical tale, "Wendy the Woodpecker Wouldn't Peck Wood." The soon to be published, "Siegel the Eagle's Olympic Dream," tells the story of a wonderfully athletic, but visually impaired eagle, and his struggles to achieve success.

The author has been married forty-two years to his wonderful wife Kathleen. They have six children and seven grandchildren, and most love the author's rhyming stories, and fondly call him, "Papa."

# About the Illustrator

Moi is a passionate Illustrator. He started his journey in illustration at a very young age, creating comics and artistic work for the entertainment of his brother and cousins. In high school, he worked as an Editorial Cartoonist. Creating art also saved his life, after he survived a very bad experience. Art is his life and identity.

Made in the USA
Monee, IL
27 September 2021